DOUBLE CUT

DOUBLE CUT

by Alfred Shaughnessy
adapted from the film *Chase a Crooked Shadow*
by David Osborn and Charles Sinclair

LONDON

A member of the Chappell and Intersong Music Group

First published 1985 by
ETG, English Theatre Guild Ltd,
129 Park Street, London W1Y 3FA.

ISBN 0 85676 021 8

Typeset and printed by Commercial Colour Press, London E7.
Cover design by Robin Lowry.
Cover photo by Frank Page.

This play was first produced at the Thorndike Theatre, Leatherhead, Surrey, on 7 February 1984, in association with Robert Fox Ltd., and by arrangement with Thomas Clyde, Douglas Fairbanks Jr. and Pamela Combemale. The cast was as follows.

CHARLES BRINTON	Charles Stapley
OLIVIA PRESCOTT	Lucy Fleming
MARIA	Lynn Webb-Turner
WARD	Simon Williams
VARGAS	Sam Dastor
CARLOS	Alkis Kritikos
ELAINE WHITMAN	Jo Ross

Directed by Roger Clissold
Designed by Stuart Stanley

The action of the play takes place in a villa on the Costa del Sol.

ACT I

Scene 1 Night.
Scene 2 Morning.

ACT II

Scene 1 Evening.
Scene 2 Morning.

Photo by Frank Page from the Thorndike Theatre Production

ACT ONE

Scene One

Scene — the luxurious living room of the Villa Rosita on the Costa Del Sol, not far from Marbella.

The old house, built on high ground near the sea, has had some recent alterations, especially the two large glass-panelled sliding doors, which are framed in a wrought iron design of Spanish character. They lead out on to the terrace, which has steps down to the swimming pool and the boathouse. The front door leads to the driveway below. There are two other doors: A single swing door to the kitchen and servants' quarters. The other is to OLIVIA*'s bedroom. A staircase leads up to the other bedrooms.*

The furniture is a mixture of Spanish exuberance and modern comfort. Pictures, wall hangings and mirrors are a similar mixture. Included is a baby grand piano, a music centre, a desk, telephone, various chairs, tables and a sofa. Empty glasses, used plates and full ashtrays litter the room to denote the aftermath of a dinner party.

Over the pre-curtain Spanish music, as it fades away and immediately preceding curtain rise, we hear cars starting up and voices saying goodnight.

At curtain rise the front door is open. MARIA, OLIVIA*'s sturdy Spanish maid, is busy clearing up ashtrays, etc., on to a tray.*

A man and a woman with their backs to the audience are seeing off their guests. These are CHARLES BRINTON*, a greying, distinguished looking architect of mature age, who has never married; and* OLIVIA PRESCOTT*, a smartly dressed young woman, attractive with the self-assurance that comes with great wealth. She is wearing an expensive decollete evening dress and a glittering diamond necklace with an emerald pendant. She looks a bit strained.*

OLIVIA (*To departing guests outside*) . . . so glad you could come . . . goodnight Miguel. Oh, please do . . .

CHARLES (*Also calling out*) . . . don't forget the left turn at the bottom of the road . . . there's a signpost for Marbella . . . corner of the vineyard . . . four kilometres.

OLIVIA . . . not at all. Loved seeing you . . . Goodnight, Inez . . . Yes, we will. I'll call you.

The last car drives away and there is a silence. OLIVIA *closes the front door and follows* CHARLES *back into the hall.* CHARLES *stifles a yawn.*

CHARLES Well, that seemed to go off all right, (*looks at watch*) What have we got it to? My God, it's one o'clock. Time I was on my way.

OLIVIA Don't go just yet. Have a nightcap. I'll fix you a nice whisky and soda.

CHARLES I shouldn't but I will, if you press me.

OLIVIA *moves up to the drinks trolley.*

CHARLES A weak one with plenty of ice. The Policía have a nasty habit of patrolling the Marbella road at night. (*Pause*) You must be tired.

OLIVIA Not really. I don't call one o'clock late, not by Johannesburg standards.

OLIVIA *hands* CHARLES *his drink.*

CHARLES Not by Spanish standards either, but I'm not exactly in the first flush of youth . . . need my sleep. (*Sips drink*) Do you know I can remember sending *you* off to bed at seven, once upon a time.

OLIVIA Did you?

CHARLES When your dear mother refused to be firm with you.

OLIVIA *smiles and takes a drink herself.*

OLIVIA I liked your friend José . . . what's his name . . . the Marquis de Something.

CHARLES José de las Rivas. Did you? He's not a bad old stick. Crazy about deep-sea fishing.

OLIVIA So I gathered.

CHARLES He has a tiresome habit of ringing me up at the crack of dawn after a late party to suggest a day's fishing in his boat. Come to think of it, he may call me early this morning . . . said he might, God help me.

OLIVIA Then take you phone off the hook. That's what I always do, if I want to sleep in. He'll give up after a bit and ask someone else.

CHARLES Good idea, I'll take your advice.

OLIVIA — But don't oversleep and forget to call for me tomorrow.

CHARLES — Ah, yes. I promised you lunch at the Puerto Banus, did I not? Quite right. (*He looks round the Villa*) Olivia, my dear, you must go easy on the social racket, you know. Remember you came here to rest.

OLIVIA — You suggested the dinner party; I didn't. A house-warming, you said. And a chance to meet my new neighbours.

CHARLES — You're quite right. I didn't want you to be lonely here, all on your own. But I warn you, the pace round this part of the coast is pretty hot. Cocktail parties, fishing picnics, barbecues, just don't want you overdoing it, after what you've been through.

OLIVIA — Stop treating me like an invalid, Uncle Charles. I'm perfectly all right now.

CHARLES — Are you?

OLIVIA — Yes, I am.

CHARLES — I'd like to see a little more colour in those cheeks.

OLIVIA — The sunshine will take care of that. (*She darts a look at* MARIA, *who is about to go out with a tray of glasses*) Leave that now and go to bed, Maria.

MARIA — Si, Señorita.

OLIVIA — And don't wake me in the morning. I'll sleep in.

MARIA — Very good, Señorita. Buenas noches, Señor, Señorita . . .

CHARLES — Buenas noches, Maria.

Maria goes. A silence.

OLIVIA — It's a year next Thursday, did you know? Since Daddy . . .

CHARLES — (*Quietly*) Yes, it must be.

OLIVIA — Why, Uncle Charles?

CHARLES — It was put down to business worries, wasn't it? Financial pressures, all that.

OLIVIA ... and the shock after Ward was ...

CHARLES No. I don't believe it had anything to do with your brother.

A pause.

OLIVIA When I arrived here last week, there was an enormous picture of me on the front cover of a Spanish magazine. (*She holds up a magazine on a table*) Had to buy it, of course. (*She puts it down again*).

CHARLES I know. I saw it too.

OLIVIA I'm not sure I like being described as a 'wealthy South African heiress'.

CHARLES Yes. That was most unfortunate. An open invitation to some scruffy little terrorist to kidnap you for a king's ransom.

OLIVIA Well, now they've got a King here once more, maybe he'd pay it and set me free. Otherwise, I can always shoot him.

CHARLES (*Shocked*) Shoot King Carlos? But he's sweet.

OLIVIA Shoot the terrorist.

CHARLES With what?

OLIVIA *goes to open a drawer of the desk and produces an automatic with a silencer.*

CHARLES My God, have you got a licence for that?

OLIVIA I've had it ever since someone broke into our house at Roseville three years ago and killed our Bantu cook. Father bought us both one and we were shown how to use them by the local police inspector.

CHARLES I'd keep it under your pillow, if I were you.

OLIVIA Would you? (*She shrugs, puts the gun back in the drawer and closes it.*) I haven't really thanked you properly for all you've done to the Villa, especially my bathroom and those sliding windows. You must send the trustees your account.

CHARLES What for?

OLIVIA Your architect's fee, of course.

CHARLES Certainly not. That was a little recovery present for my sister Rose's favourite child.

OLIVIA (*Kisses him*) Thanks, Uncle Charles. You're a doll.

CHARLES Well, I must be on my way. Take care, my dear.

He moves to the door.

OLIVIA You drive carefully and watch out for the Policía.

CHARLES I always do. See you tommorrow.

OLIVIA I'll be ready.

CHARLES *goes out.* OLIVIA *stands at the door until he has driven away. Then she closes the front door, bolting and chaining it. She switches off some lights and moves down to the drinks trolley to finish her drink. On an impulse she puts a cassette on the music centre and presses the button. We hear a section of Ravel's Violincello Concerto.* OLIVIA *takes her drink out on to the terrace by the sliding glass panels, which are still open and stands looking up at the Spanish night. Then, feeling a bit chilled, she comes in again and is about to slide the panels shut, when a sound over by the front door makes her turn and listen. Footsteps can be heard crunching slowly on the gravel drive below, then coming up the steps.* OLIVIA *switches off the cassette and goes over to the front door, listens again. The footsteps have ceased. Puzzled she unbolts the front door again, opening it an inch or two in spite of the chain. She peers out.*

OLIVIA Maria? Is that you? Maria. Is there somebody out there? Who is it?

Evidently OLIVIA *can see nobody, so she closes the front door again and bolts it. As she does so a man can be seen crossing the terrace outside. He walks in through the still open glass windows.* OLIVIA, *turning from the front door sees him and gasps. The man is well dressed bronzed, good-looking and a year or two older than* OLIVIA.

MAN Good evening, Olivia.

OLIVIA *looks baffled and a touch scared.*

OLIVIA Who the hell are you?

MAN I think you know who I am.

OLIVIA I most certainly do not. (*Pause*) Are you a reporter? Because, if you are, I must ask you to . . .

MAN Olivia, please. You know as well as I do that I am not a reporter, and never have been.

OLIVIA Look, I know there's just been a party here and I haven't finished locking up . . . if you've dropped in hoping for a free drink, I'm afraid you're out of luck; the party's over, everyone's gone, so . . . (*Suddenly sharp*) How do you know my name?

MAN I'd like a drink, please. Party or no party.

OLIVIA Get out. Just clear off, will you or I'll call the police.

MAN The same old Olivia.

The man moves further into the room. OLIVIA goes to the telephone on the desk, picks it up, and dials zero.

OLIVIA (*Into phone*) Oiga . . . policía urgente. Villa Rosita . . . si . . .

MAN (*Talking over* OLIVIA'*s muttered conversation*) Yes, that's quite a glamorous picture of you on the front cover of this month's 'Olé'. (*He picks up magazine and reads from it translating from the Spanish*). I like the story inside too. Nice touching stuff. 'Attractive Olivia Prescott, the tragic 'heredera de diamantes', that's diamond heiress to you . . . arrived this week at the luxury Villa Rosita on the Costa del Sol left to her by her South African father, diamond magnate McKenzie Prescott, who committed 'suicidio' in Johannesburg last year . . .

OLIVIA (*Into phone*) Policía? Prescott. Villa Rosita . . . si un hombre desconocido ha entrado . . . en mi casa y no quiere marcharse . . . si . . . Quién? . . . Si, ciertamente . . . Prescott Villa Rosita . . . gracias.

OLIVIA *hangs up. The man puts down the magazine.*

OLIVIA The Police will be here in a few minutes. They're out on Patrol along this road. Don't you want to go before they get here?

MAN No, I don't think so. I'd rather stay and talk to you. By the way, was that Uncle Charles I saw leaving just now? May I? (*He pours himself a whisky.* OLIVIA *just stares at the man unbelieving.*) Nice of him to have this Villa fixed up for you. But then Uncle Charles always was a pretty good foster-uncle to the Prescott children over the years . . .

OLIVIA You've done your homework well, haven't you? I suppose that's how cons like you operate. Watch the papers for the obituary notices of rich men, find out who gets the money and move in. Well, you're not going to con me, so I'd go home, if I were you and find someone else to latch on to. Someone dull and stupid.

MAN Ah, come on, Olivia, don't tell me you're never conned. How about the Belgian tennis pro you fell for that summer in Monte Carlo when you were nineteen?

OLIVIA *is speechless and bewildered.*

MAN I haven't asked you how you are, by the way. Recovered from your . . . well, over the shock by now, I hope. Must have been quite a trauma for you. All those weeks following Father's untimely death. The South African newspapers made rather a meal of it, didn't they? But then . . .

OLIVIA (*Quietly*) Who the hell are you? What is this all about?

MAN ... of course Father *was* President of the Transvaal Diamond Corporation and a prominent citizen of ...

OLIVIA (*Screaming*) Shut up. I won't listen to any more of this ... get out!

MAN Oh, dear. I'm sorry. Didn't realize you were still upset, not after a whole year. I'm so sorry.

A silence, as OLIVIA *keeps her ears blocked up. Then there is a knock. The man makes no move. Just stands his ground.* OLIVIA *gets up and looks over towards the front door. Outside a blue police lamp is flashing.*

MAN Your visitors from the Policía, no doubt. Aren't you going to let them in?

OLIVIA *darts a look at the man, then goes up to open the front door to Comisario* VARGAS *and a* GUARDIA. VARGAS *is a sharp, wily, middle-aged man with penetrating eyes.*

OLIVIA Señor Comisario?

VARGAS Si, Señorita ... Vargas.

OLIVIA Please come in.

They do so, OLIVIA *closes the door. The* GUARDIA *remains by the door.*

OLIVIA I'm sorry to call you so late; thank you for coming.

VARGAS Where is intruder, please? The man that you say broke into your house?

VARGAS *glances at the man, whom he assumes to be a husband or guest, as he stands very composed and calm, sipping his drink.* OLIVIA *looks hard at the man.*

OLIVIA He refuses to go and there's only my maid, who lives over the garage ... and ...

VARGAS I understand, Señorita: but I do not see intruder.

OLIVIA (*Points to the man*) It's this man here ... He just walked in ... from the terrace.

MAN Come on, Olivia, cut it out, for God's sake. What's the game?

VARGAS I shall ask the questions, Señor.

OLIVIA I just want this man taken away, out of my villa, that's all. I'm very tired and I want to go to bed.

MAN Not too tired for silly games, it seems. You really ought to be spanked. Naughty Olivia. (*To* VARGAS) Sorry about all this. I'd go now, if I were you. False alarm.

For a while he looks from one to the other, assessing the situation.

VARGAS I shall leave, Señor, only when I have checked the young lady's complaint. Your credentials, if you please, Señor; you have some means of identification?

The man looks indignant. Then he looks at OLIVIA.

MAN All right, Olivia. If you want to play the fool and waste this officer's time, I'm easy. (*The man gets out his wallet, as* VARGAS *moves over to him, and hands the Police Comisario various documents for inspection*) My international driving licence, a Letter of Credit from the Union Bank of South Africa.

VARGAS May I see your passport, please?

MAN My . . .

For a second OLIVIA *looks triumphant.*

VARGAS Passport.

MAN Ah, yes, of course.

The man brings out a passport from his pocket, and hands it to VARGAS.

VARGAS (*To* OLIVIA) I do not know who is playing games in the middle of the night but whoever it is . . . we do not like . . . (VARGAS *is now examining the man's passport and comparing his face with the photo*) people who try to make fools of the Policía . . .

VARGAS *hands the passport open to* OLIVIA.

OLIVIA (*Tense*) What are you talking about?

OLIVIA *looks at the passport.*

VARGAS The name of your intruder appears to be Mr Ward McKenzie Prescott. And you are Miss Prescott, I believe.

OLIVIA But this is absurd . . . my brother's dead.

VARGAS Dead.

WARD *strolls casually across the room.*

WARD I really must apologize for my sister, Inspector: I'm afraid she's inherited our mutual father's fondness for practical jokes. April Fool's Day was a nightmare when we were kids: wasn't it, Olivia? You never knew what he was going to . . .

OLIVIA (*Quietly*)My brother is dead.

VARGAS One moment, please. Allow me to conduct the enquiries. (*To* WARD) Now, Señor, since the Señorita telephoned us in the first place to make a complaint, I must first question you about yourself. You are a resident of Spain?

WARD No, I've just arrived over here from Johannesburg; drove down today from Madrid. When I got here . . .

OLIVIA (*Shouting*) Liar . . . he's lying . . . I've told you my brother's dead.

VARGAS Señorita, please.

OLIVIA You don't understand. My brother, Ward, Ward McKenzie Prescott is no longer alive. For God's sake. I should know!

VARGAS I'm sorry, Señorita but dead men do not carry valid passports. Why did you insist on this foolishness in the middle of the night . . . was it perhaps a result of entertaining here . . . there were guests, I believe. And perhaps much wine was consumed . . .

OLIVIA How dare you say that?

WARD I'm sorry you've had this trouble, Inspector. I'll make sure my sister doesn't bother you again

VARGAS *turns to leave but* OLIVIA *takes hold of his arm, desperate.*

OLIVIA No, please don't go. You must listen to me at least hear my side . . . look my brother Ward was killed a year ago in South Africa the night before my Father died. I swear it on my honour his car went off the road and turned over . . . I . . . I . . . should know. I saw the . . . body . . . I had to identify it.

VARGAS *pauses, turns and listens to her.*

OLIVIA There was a double family funeral at the Cathedral in Pretoria for him and my father . . . all our friends were there, photographs in the papers, everything.

VARGAS I would prefer to believe you, Señorita, but I must believe what I see. This gentleman has identified himself to my satisfaction with his passport.

OLIVIA That's not by brother's photograph.

VARGAS You have others?

OLIVIA In my bedroom, I'll go and fetch . . .

VARGAS No. Remain here, please. The Guardia will find it.

VARGAS *speaks to the* GUARDIA *muttering something about a photograph in Spanish. The* GUARDIA *goes off to* OLIVIA*'s bedroom.*

VARGAS (*To* WARD) How long since you have seen your sister?

OLIVIA (*Quietly*) I'm not his sister . . .

WARD Not for over a year . . . just before the car accident.

VARGAS Ah, there was an accident.

WARD — Yes but I wasn't in it. You see I'd given a lift to a man, who flagged me down on the road that evening. As it turned out, he took *me* for a ride. Hit me over the head, stole my wallet, chucked me out and drove off in my car.

OLIVIA — Look, if you have no objection, Señor Comisario, I'm going to call my uncle, Mr Brinton, the architect: he was here earlier on. His villa's just outside San Pedro de Alcantara. He'll soon tell you who's lying.

OLIVIA *has picked up the phone and is dialling a number. We hear an engaged signal.*

VARGAS — (*To* WARD) Señor Prescott, if these things happened many months ago . . .

WARD — I was still unconscious, when they found me. Matter of fact I was in hospital for months with a fractured skull.

OLIVIA *hangs up and dials again, frustrated.*

WARD — (*To* VARGAS) It's all there in the hospital records, if you care to check . . .

OLIVIA — (*At phone*) Operator? San Pedro . . . tres . . . uno . . . uno . . . seis . . . si (*Pause*) Ocupado? Oh God. Well, will you have it tested please? I know he's there.

VARGAS has come up to OLIVIA and reaches for the phone. She hands it to him.

VARGAS — (*Into phone*)El Comisario Vargas . . . Policía . . . si. Pruebe la linea del Señor . . .

He looks at OLIVIA *enquiringly.*

OLIVIA — Charles Brinton.

VARGAS — Señor Charles Brinton, si . . . por favor. (*To* OLIVIA) They will check again. (*The phone can be heard ringing out the engaged signal. Into phone*) Cuánto tiempo? . . . Gracias, Señorita . . . (VARGAS *hangs up the phone*) The line is out of order unless possibly the receiver has not been replaced.

OLIVIA Oh, God . . . yes . . . of course . . . that's what he's done. He's gone to sleep with the phone off the hook. He said he might. (*Brokenly*) Oh hell! What can I do?

The GUARDIA *comes in again with a photograph in a frame, which he hands to* WARD *who glances at it and hands it to* OLIVIA. *She looks at it and reacts violently, turning on* WARD.

OLIVIA Very clever. I might have guessed you'd make sure of that too. I suppose you had it taken specially for this little adventure.

VARGAS If there is no other way that you can prove to us this gentleman is not your brother, as he claims, I regret there is no more that I can do tonight, Señorita.

OLIVIA (*Suddenly*) Wait. I've thought of someting. Just ask him to show you the small anchor tattooed on his left wrist. My brother had one.

WARD Olivia, really. You're going much too far.

OLIVIA Go on, show him. Show your anchor. If you've got one.

VARGAS You have a tattoo mark on your wrist?

WARD *quickly pulls up his sleeve. He displays a small anchor tattooed on his wrist to* VARGAS.

WARD Had that done for a dare after a wild party at Wits (*Pronounced 'Vits'*)

VARGAS Wits?

WARD Witwatersrand. My old university. Johannesburg's number one seat of learning. (*Rolling back his sleeve*) Come on, Olivia, I think the Inspector's had enough of this nonsense, don't you? (OLIVIA *moves over to* WARD) Can't you see you're wasting the poor man's time?

OLIVIA *suddenly slashes* WARD *across the face with her hand.* VARGAS *grabs hold of her to restrain her.*

VARGAS Stop that. It is enough for one night. Señorita. I do not wish to arrest you for wasting the time of the police; but I shall be obliged to, if you continue this behaviour.

WARD (*Rubbing his face*) It's all right, don't be hard on her, Inspector. If I hadn't written to tell her I was arriving from South Africa, she'd have had no chance to plan this rather childish little charade.

VARGAS Do not worry, Señor Prescott. I shall not arrest the Señoria for what appears to be a private family joke.

OLIVIA, *irritated once more picks up the phone, and dials.* WARD *takes* VARGAS *by the arm confidentially.*

WARD Trouble is, my sister's hopelessly spoilt. Always had her own way; father doted on her. Also, she's extremely neurotic.

VARGAS So I can see.

WARD . . . not been at all well. Under a lot of strain this last year . . . have to make allowances for her.

VARGAS I understand, Señor. You will call me if I can be of any further assistance.

WARD I will. Thank you for coming up and my apologies.

VARGAS *goes out,* WARD *closes the door behind him.* OLIVIA *is still on the phone. The engaged tone goes on and on.* WARD *strolls back into the hall, very cool.*

WARD Uncles Charles' line still unobtainable? Pity. I feel like another drink. Should have offered the Comisario one, shouldn't I? Failing in my duties as a host. (*Looking around*) I always liked this villa, you know, but then Father knew how to spend his money well. I should have put in more time here. And less on my motor racing.

OLIVIA *slams down the phone and now stands beside it, watching* WARD *as he strolls about, pushing at the trolley to pour himself a drink.*

OLIVIA Why didn't you?

WARD No, seriously. I should have made the effort. Father would have appreciated it.

OLIVIA Yes, I can imagine.

WARD They say he always knew how to make the best of a fine diamond. How to set it. This place is a perfect setting for you Olivia. Spain, the coast, this villa, the old man knew what he was doing, buying a property on the highest point for miles around. I only wish he was still with us to enjoy it. But he isn't, is he? There's just the two of us now. Just you and I. (WARD *sips his drink*)

OLIVIA One good reason you're not my brother is that you're too bloody clever. Ward wasn't brainy at all, just good at driving fast cars round and round in circles. You . . . you're dead clever, aren't you? The way you've planned all this, got hold of all that detailed information; but I know what you're after, I wasn't born yesterday. I just hope you realize what a gamble you're taking. (WARD *just smiles patiently*) You think you can keep up this ridiculous pretence for a few days, so that no one will interfere, when you help your 'sister' to dispose of her valuable jewellery. That's it, isn't it? (WARD *says nothing*) OK I'll negotiate. I'm not proud. Let's make a deal, shall we? (OLIVIA *takes off the diamond necklace with emerald pendant round her neck and hands it to* WARD) Here you are. It's insured against theft; take it and get out.

WARD My dear Olivia, what is the matter with you? The police have gone now, the joke's over. (WARD *strolls over to the baby grand piano whose lid is open from the party. He begins to strum a tune*) Remember this? The bar of that beach hotel up the coast from Durban three years ago . . . that American pianist used to play it over and over again for you. We called him 'Sam', remember?

OLIVIA All right. What do you want? You're not my brother, so you must be here for something. If it's me you're after, you could have raped me any time during the last few minutes. So it can't be that. You've refused a priceless piece of jewellery. So what the hell is it?

Suddenly OLIVIA *dashes for the front door, which has been left unbolted, and runs out.* WARD *makes no attempt to stop her. Instead he sits at the piano and strums on. After a time* OLIVIA *comes back in, dejected.*

OLIVIA Where are the keys of my car?

WARD Never leave keys in cars, Olivia, especially at night. Very bad habit. Here. (WARD *pauses in his playing to hand her the keys*) Take them. Go on. You're not a prisoner here. Drive away into the night, if you wish to.

OLIVIA *takes the car keys and looks at them, then at him. She goes off into her bedroom.* WARD *goes on strumming the piano. After a bit she comes out in a light belted overcoat with a Gucci shoulder bag slung over one shoulder. She pauses, looks at* WARD. *He ignores her, goes on playing. She looks over towards the front door. Makes up her mind and goes to open it. She is about to go out into the night, when* WARD *stops playing. She hesitates.*

WARD It wouldn't be very sensible, you know. I'd simply have you brought back. (WARD *crosses to her at the door, as she turns to face him. As he speaks he unbuttons her coat, which she allows him to do.*) And that could mean hospital again. (*He tries to take her bag but she clings on to it*)

OLIVIA (*Weakly*) Hospital?

WARD The clinic for nervous disorders. All those specialists and sedatives, when you had to be kept in darkened rooms . . .

OLIVIA *meekly stands there in her unbuttoned coat, clutching her bag.*

WARD I'm only going by what I heard. After Father's death and all the trouble with the company, it was quite understandable. Poor old Olivia, you've been through it, haven't you? Acute anxiety, isn't that what they called it?

OLIVIA I want't ill.

WARD The doctors seemed to think you were. And they'd think so again, Olivia. You're not over it yet. So why not accept the fact that you're still under a great strain, especially after entertaining all those people this evening. Why not sit down and have a cigarette?

WARD *proffers a gold cigarette case*

OLIVIA (*Irritable*) No, thank you. (*Noticing the case*) Where did you get that?

WARD This? You gave it to me, didn't you? For my 21st birthday

OLIVIA That't Ward's.

WARD Yes. And I treasure it. Always will.

OLIVIA *looks for a moment at* WARD, *then she lets out a desperate cry of fear and dashes into her bedroom slamming the door. We hear the key turn in the lock and a muffled sound of sobbing inside.* WARD, *calm and cool, goes slowly over to pick up the phone on the desk. Operator answers.*

WARD (*Into phone*) Marbella Dos, Cuatro, Tres, Seis, Uno. Si (*Pause*) Hotel Dominga? Cuarto ochenta. Gracias. (*English*) Hello. Yes, it's me. Get out here as soon as you can. Yes, at once. Turn off at Kilometre Post 101. I'll be waiting for you.

As WARD *hangs up, the lights fade.*

Scene Two

The next morning. Lights fade up with bright Spanish sunshine, beginning to cloud over. WARD *can be seen out on the terrace in sunglasses, very cool and calm as usual, finishing his breakfast and reading a copy of 'The Iberian Sun'.*

OLIVIA*'s bedroom door is unlocked and opens slowly and cautiously.* OLIVIA *peeps out. She is tousled after a troubled night and in her dressing gown. Finding the hall empty and not seeing* WARD *out on the terrace, she* *makes for the stairs and calls out in a tense, controlled voice:*

OLIVIA Maria . . . Maria . . . oiga. Venga Aqui . . .

Getting no reply, she moves to the pass door through to the servants' quarters, kitchen etc. and opens it quickly. She jumps back with shock to find a strange Spanish manservant, CARLOS, *standing there. He is rather grim-faced and wearing a white, short jacket.*

OLIVIA Who are you?

Before the man can answer a strange woman appears on the stairs. She is MRS WHITMAN; *English, practical and handsome; about* WARD*'s age.*

MRS WHITMAN (*Coming down*) His name is Carlos, Miss Prescott. The new manservant, and I'm Elaine Whitman. A friend of your brother's.

OLIVIA Where's my maid?

MRS WHITMAN Ward sent Maria home to her family for a few days.

WARD *now comes in from the terrace with two cups of coffee, handing one to* OLIVIA.

WARD (*Cheerful*) Morning, Olivia. Marvellous day. Mrs Whitman's come to stay with us for a while. Old friend of mine. I'm sure you'll get on together. Carlos will get you some breakfast, if you want anything; had mine, I'm afraid, but I'll join you for a cup of coffee.

OLIVIA (*Sullen*) I don't eat breakfast, thank you. (*Takes coffee and sips it*) It's gone eleven anyway. Uncle Charles is coming to pick me up for lunch, you know. He should be very happy to see you here, you and your . . . guest.

CARLOS *goes off.*

MRS WHITMAN Oh, I'm so sorry, Miss Prescott. I forgot to mention it, Mr Brinton telephoned early this morning. He apologizes but he can't take you to lunch today; he has an important client to see.

WARD You've been stood up. Too bad.

Mrs Whitman *goes off through the staff door.*

Olivia (*With suppressed rage*) Well . . . (*She moves to the windows to glance out*) . . . since I'm apparently not lunching out after all, I might as well have a swim. If I have your permission.

Ward I say (Ward *now points to an oil painting on the wall*) That's new, isn't it? Where'd you get it?

Olivia *glances at the picture.*

Olivia In Paris. Ward gave it to me the summer before last . . . he was my brother, you know. He picked it up in a little shop on the banks of the Seine down by the Pont Neuf.

Ward Really?

Olivia That's right.

Ward How extraordinary.

Olivia Why?

Ward I was in Rome for the whole of the summer before last Olivia, staying with the Pavrolinis. Haven't set foot in Paris for three years.

Olivia *looks at him, baffled as ever. Then,*

Olivia No. You wouldn't have, would you? Well, I'm going to change for my swim. (Olivia *moves off towards her bedroom*) Fix me a drink, will you?

Ward Isn't it a little early in the day?

Olivia (*Pausing*) That doesn't sound much like Ward Prescott.

Ward I've had to watch myself . . . since the accident. What'll it be?

Olivia Why, Mr Prescott, you surprise me. Can't you guess?

Ward *look a bit thrown.*

Olivia My swimming drink, of course. Same as I've always had before a swim for the last ten years . . .

OLIVIA *goes into her bedroom, leaving the door open, so she can talk through.* WARD *starts to look on the trolley for various bottles and ingredients.*

WARD (*Calling out*) Just remind me what we called it . . . A bushveldt Vodka, was it . . . or a Joburg Ginsling . . . or

OLIVIA (*Off*) It was just called our 'pool stinger'. Surely you remember that.

WARD Yes, I do, now you come to mention it. (WARD *is now tentatively opening various bottles and mixing a concoction in a shaker with slight apprehension*) I remember the first time I fixed you one. You were only sixteen, not supposed to drink; but it was your birthday and you had some of your school-friends over to swim. I fixed you a . . . 'pool stinger' and squeezed it into your hand just before we all want over to the pool. Funny how little things stick in the mind.

OLIVIA *now emerges in a beach-robe over her bikini.*

OLIVIA Yes, don't they? Now how about my drink?

WARD *has completed the complicated cocktail and pours one from the shaker.*

WARD (*Handing glass*) Try it. Not too much Cassis?

OLIVIA No.

WARD Not too much soda?

OLIVIA No. It's exactly the way Ward made it. Exactly. You really are very clever. 'If on my theme I rightly think, there are five reasons why I drink . . .'

WARD (*After a fractional hesitation*) . . . 'Good wine, a friend, because I'm dry or lest I should be bye and bye . . .

TOGETHER . . . or any other reason why . . .'

OLIVIA *laughs drily but with growing alarm.*

OLIVIA So you know out toast too. O.K. So Ward Prescott is somehow back from the dead. In quest of the Prescott fortune, one must presume.

Well, I have to tell you that it's not as vast as it used to be. As for the Prescott name . . . that's a little tarnished I'm afraid. This Villa? You seem to like it here. Is it the Villa you want? Or what?

WARD says nothing, just looks at her with his maddening faint smile. She turns, putting her drink down and goes to the glass windows.

OLIVIA All right. I shall go and have my swim now, if you've no objection. I'd rather take some exercise than sit in here all day listening to a pack of lies.

OLIVIA goes angrily out on to the terrace and away to the pool. MRS WHITMAN comes in from the kitchen area.

WARD Our 'poor little rich girl' is sulking, I'm afraid.

MRS WHITMAN They are inclined to.

WARD We can't keep her here indefinitely.

MRS WHITMAN Has she got the keys of her car?

WARD Yes, but she knows better than to try it.

MRS WHITMAN How about the launch?

WARD Possible. I'll go down to the boathouse and immobilize it, before we go into the town.

There is a distant rumble of thunder outside.

MRS WHITMAN How soon before she'll be ready to . . . sh . . . she's coming back.

WARD gestures MRS WHITMAN to be quiet, seeing OLIVIA returning up the steps and in from the terrace. OLIVIA walks in again, tightlipped and angry.

OLIVIA Who the hell gave orders for the pool to be emptied?

WARD Carlos was instructed to drain it early this morning; it needs to be properly cleaned out. Besides, there are thunderstorms about in the hills. All the same, I should have remembered to tell you. I'm so sorry. Now, if you'll excuse us, we have things to do in Marbella.

OLIVIA What things?

WARD Some cables to send and telex messages. We shan't be long. Carlos will be here to make sure you don't . . .

OLIVIA Don't what? Make a run for it?

WARD To see you don't lack the service and attention due to a woman of your wealth and position. That's all.

WARD *moves towards the front door.*

OLIVIA Why do you have to send your cables from Marbella, when there's a perfectly good telephone here.

WARD Their contents are somewhat sensitive and confidential. Come on, Elaine. Before the storm breaks and floods the road.

WARD *and* MRS WHITMAN *go off through the front door. Then another rumble of thunder a bit closer and* OLIVIA *looks out of the windows, turning suddenly away as a flash of light almost blinds her. The storm breaks now, good and proper, crashes of thunder and flashes of lightning outside. The pass door opens and* CARLOS, *the manservant, peers in, sees* OLIVIA *sobbing though she doesn't see him. He goes out again, his expression impassive and cold.* OLIVIA *recovers a bit, tries to pull herself together and goes slowly over to the telephone to dial for the operator once more.*

OLIVIA (*Into phone*) . . . por favor . . . San Pedro . . . Uno, treis, treis, uno . . . si (*We hear the odd long drawn out, high pitched ringing out tone. Then a Spanish woman's voice answers*) (*Into phone*) . . . hallo . . . the house of Mr Brinton. Ah. Miss Prescott to speak to him . . . he when? Oh, God. All day, I see. When do you expect him back? Oh . . . Yes, it's very urgent. His niece . . . Yes, please, as soon as he can . . . Thank you

OLIVIA *hangs up, despondent. Another crash of thunder, followed by a loud knocking at the front door.* OLIVIA, *alarmed, goes to the pass door to call through.*

OLIVIA (*Calling through*) Carlos . . . the door. There's someone at the front door. Will you see who it is, please?

CARLOS *appears in his white jacket and slowly goes over to open the door. On the door step stands Comisario* VARGAS, *dripping wet in a cape.*

VARGAS Esta la Señorita Prescott en casa?

CARLOS *hesitates but* OLIVIA *sees* VARGAS.

OLIVIA Yes, I'm here. Come in, please. (*To* CARLOS) It's all right, Carlos. Show the Señor Comisario in, please.

CARLOS *bows and goes off.* VARGAS *comes into the hall, shaking his wet cape and hat.*

OLIVIA Why have you come back? I thought you'd washed your hands of my case.

VARGAS A routine visit, Señorita. Is your intruder still with you?

OLIVIA Do you mean my dead brother? The walking corpse?

VARGAS (*Drily*) I mean the gentleman who was here last night.

OLIVIA No. He's not. He's gone into Marbella, with his accomplice. A woman, needless to say. She turned up sometime during the night. I'm sure they'll be back later.

VARGAS And you are still saying this man is not your brother?

OLIVIA Of course I am; and I'm wondering how much longer you're going to allow this outrageous breach of the law to go on with a strange man trespassing in my house.

VARGAS The gentleman has not broken the law.

OLIVIA Nonsense. There must be some law to get him off my private property. If there isn't, then it's high time there was. Now, are you going to throw him out of here or must I get on to our Embassy in Madrid?

VARGAS If the villa belonged only to you . . . but he is your . . .

OLIVIA No. You keep saying that . . . I'm telling you he is NOT. Do you think I'd ask the police to arrest my own brother in my own house and have him slung into jail? What do you think the Press would make of that? I'd be front-page news everywhere. For God's sake why should I keep denying it, if it's true; for what possible purpose? He's an imposter and a con man out for money and . . . (*Suddenly pathetic*) . . . you must believe me . . . please. I'm not crazy . . . I'm perfectly sane, and very scared.

VARGAS (*Quietly*) You do not make it easy for me, Señorita. I should like to believe you. I very much wish to help; but tell me something unlawful he has done. Has he . . . stolen anything? Has he struck you or threatened you in any way?

OLIVIA No. That's just the point. I don't know what he wants . . . He won't say. He just smiles and goes on treating me as his sister (*Sudden anger again*) . . . look you've got to get rid of him. After all, isn't that what the police are for? To protect people from this sort of thing.

VARGAS Unfortunately, things are not so simple, Señorita. From my point of view he is a foreign visitor. He comes to this country with his passport, and other credentials, all perfectly in order. It would seem he is a man of wealth and influence. Now what do I do? Throw him into prison and create as you say an international scandal with consulates and embassy officials complaining and many awkward questions for my government?

OLIVIA But there must be dozens of things you can do. Records can be looked up, official records. The death certificate in South Africa, for instance. My brother's death certificate.

VARGAS Based on your identification of the body found in his car after the crash. Yours alone?

OLIVIA I know what you're going say. Well, it was Ward. It just . . . was.

VARGAS Not the man who knocked him out, stole his wallet, and drove away in his car?

OLIVIA All that's a lie. It's just not true. Look, why are you so ready to believe what this man says, this crook? You glance casually at his passport, and his papers and, just because there's a photograph and a lot of rubber stamping and signatures, you accept it. Why shouldn't it all be forged?

The rain has stopped. Sunshine again.

VARGAS Why not; but also why? People with forged passports do not usually behave as your . . . as this man is behaving. I have made enquiries at the Bank this morning, Señorita Prescott. The gentleman's letter of credit is perfectly genuine. As a rule banks are most particular about these matters. So you see, I am being logical. I must be.

OLIVIA *is choking back her rage.*

OLIVIA It's quite obvious you have no intention of helping me. All right, if you choose to leave me at the mercy of this maniac . . .

VARGAS (*With a shrug*) You must try to appreciate my position, Señorita. The Policía can only deal with crimes that are actually committed. Not with crimes that are imagined.

He goes to the front door.

OLIVIA Very well. If I'm found later today with my throat cut and all my jewellery missing, it'll be your bloody fault.

VARGAS I shall take that chance, Señorita.

VARGAS *goes out.* OLIVIA *watches him go, then moves, more despondent than ever, to lock and chain the front door and fasten the glass window. Then she goes into her room closing the door. The telephone rings. Instantly* CARLOS *comes swiftly through the pass door and goes straight up to the phone to pick it up.* OLIVIA *also hurries to the phone but* CARLOS *is there first.*

OLIVIA No, Carlos. Leave it. I'll answer it.

She is too late. CARLOS *already has the receiver.*

CARLOS Villa Rosita . . .

OLIVIA (*Shouting*) Put that down.

CARLOS *ignores* OLIVIA *and takes the call.*

CARLOS No, Sir, the Señora is not here. She has gone into the town. Very good, Sir, I will give her your message when she returns.

OLIVIA Who is it? Was that for me?

CARLOS *hangs up the phone and makes to go.*

OLIVIA Carlos, I'm asking you. Who was that? Answer me, will you?

CARLOS Message for Señora Whitman. Excuse, please.

OLIVIA Just a minute, Carlos.

CARLOS Señorita?

OLIVIA I want to ask you one or two questions.

CARLOS *turns back to face* OLIVIA.

OLIVIA Since this happens to be my house, and I didn't have the pleasure of engaging you myself, I should very much like to know who did.

CARLOS The English gentleman offer me employment here, Señorita. When I am interviewed at the agency in Malaga, Señora Whitman has been also present.

OLIVIA I see. So technically, your employer is . . .

CARLOS *hesitates, seeming not to understand.*

OLIVIA . . . the person who engaged you and undertook to pay your wages . . who was it?

CARLOS It was Señor Prescott.

OLIVIA Is that what he told you to call him?

CARLOS It is the gentleman's name, Señorita. The agency speak of Señor Prescott, when they confirm my engagement.

OLIVIA Your English is pretty good.

CARLOS Thank you, Señorita.

OLIVIA How long did they engage you for?

CARLOS There was agreed no time, Señorita. Two weeks notice, if my service no longer be required.

OLIVIA Who did you work for, before you came here? Were your references taken up?

CARLOS I was not in private service, Señorita.

OLIVIA Oh, I see.

CARLOS I am Assistant Head Waiter at the Hotel Dominga in Malaga. The Manager allow me to come here to work privately for Señor Prescott.

CARLOS *bows, about to go but . . .*

OLIVIA Just a minute, Carlos.

CARLOS Señorita?

OLIVIA You have a car, haven't you?

CARLOS *does not reply.*

OLIVIA Didn't I see a green Volkswagen beetle just now, when I went down to the swimming pool? Parked outside the annexe?

CARLOS *nods.*

CARLOS It is my car, Señorita.

OLIVIA I thought so. Look. Would you be prepared — for a suitable reward — a very generous reward in fact — to drive me in your car to Malaga airport?

CARLOS *ponders this for a while, then,*

CARLOS When would you be wishing to go?

OLIVIA Now; at once. Bring your car round to the front door and I'll be ready. But we'll have to be quick.

CARLOS What would be the reward, Señorita?

OLIVIA A necklace you could sell anywhere in the world for well over a million pesetas. That's a lot of money for a one way trip to Malaga Airport. But you'll have to make up your mind now. Quickly.

CARLOS I will go to change my coat, Señorita.

OLIVIA Thank God. I'll want you to avoid the coast road and go inland by the mountains . . .

CARLOS Very good, Señorita.

OLIVIA *hurries into her bedroom to get ready, leaving her door ajar.* CARLOS *watches her and as soon as she has gone in he picks op the phone and dials a number. Somebody answers.* CARLOS *speaks loud for* OLIVIA*'s benefit.*

CARLOS Es el Real Automovil Club de Espana? Informacionas, por favor . . . Quiero saber si hay indundaciones en la carreterra entre Monda y Malaga . . . Aeropuerto . . . si . . . gracias.

CARLOS *hangs up and goes out by the pass door. Almost at once* OLIVIA *emerges from her bedroom wearing her belted overcoat and headscarf, just in the act of putting her glittering pendant into her shoulder bag and closing it. She walks swiftly to the front door unbolts and unchains it and flings it open. She lets out a sharp gasp for* WARD *stands there with a bunch of flowers in his hand.*

WARD (*Casually*) Hullo. Where are you off to?

OLIVIA *is speechless for a moment.*

OLIVIA Nowhere . . . just felt like some fresh air . . . thought of going for a walk.

Without a word WARD *crosses to the piano and lays the flowers down on it.*

WARD I can't stand dead flowers.

OLIVIA (*Weakly*) Can't you?

WARD No, I can't. Time those were thrown away. I've got us some . . .

The front door opens again and CARLOS *stands there dressed in a dark jacket and a hat.* WARD *turning sees him.*

WARD Why are you dressed like that?

CARLOS The car is ready for the Señorita.

A silence. WARD *looks at* OLIVIA *then at* CARLOS. *Finally,*

WARD You can put your car away Carlos. The Señorita is not planning to go anywhere. (*To* OLIVIA) Are you?

OLIVIA *says nothing.* WARD *turns back to* CARLOS.

WARD You can go and change back into your white jacket but take this vase and empty it, throw away the dead flowers and fill it with fresh water.

CARLOS Si, Señor.

CARLOS *goes to the piano, picks up the flower vase and exits by the pass door.*

WARD Would you like to arrange these when Carlos brings the vase back? I'm not much of a hand with flowers.

OLIVIA *ignores this and goes into her bedroom slamming the door. A pause. Then* MRS WHITMAN *comes from the kitchen. She and* WARD *exchange looks and* MRS WHITMAN *goes towards the stairs. They speak in lowered voices.*

MRS WHITMAN Where is she?

WARD In her room.

MRS WHITMAN Vargas has been here.

WARD What for?

MRS WHITMAN Just a routine visit. Carlos took a call while we were out. From Louis.

WARD Oh?

MRS WHITMAN He arrived in Tangier yesterday.

WARD He'll have to lie up there, until we're ready for him.

MRS WHITMAN Yes, but we'll need him later on. To handle the legal side.

CARLOS *comes back with the vase re-filled, wearing his white jacket again. He places the vase on the piano.*

WARD Thank you, Carlos, that will be all.

CARLOS *goes off.* OLIVIA *comes in again from her bedroom minus her coat and bag.* MRS WHITMAN *looks at* OLIVIA *and goes upstairs.*

OLIVIA Someone rang up for that cow, while you were out. Carlos took the message.

WARD Did he? Well, no doubt he'll give it to her later.

OLIVIA *suddenly seems to decide on new tactics, to play along with the situation. She smiles faintly at* WARD *for the first time and starts to arrange the flowers.*

WARD You seem a little more cheerful. Are you?

OLIVIA I'm all right.

WARD You're looking better.

OLIVIA I slept will, considering everything.

WARD Good. That was sensible. No point in worrying when there's nothing to worry about.

A pause.

OLIVIA (*Tentatively*) How long are you thinking of staying here? You and your guest.

WARD That depends on you really.

OLIVIA Oh, does it?

WARD Yes, it depends on whether we manage to get your co-operation or not on a certain business matter. The sooner it can be done the sooner we shall go away and leave you in peace.

OLIVIA I see. So this Mrs Whitman is a sort of business associate of yours, is that right? A kind of partner in . . . how can I put it?

WARD Were you thinking of saying a kind of 'partner in crime'?

OLIVIA Yes. I bloody well was.

WARD (*Sharp*) No crime has been committed nor is any crime about to be committed.

OLIVIA You stroll in here, out of the night, take the keys from my car so I can't escape, get rid of my maid while I'm asleep, and install your 'business associate' plus a creepy Spanish man servant who looks more like an ETA terrorist than a butler. Then you have the nerve to tell me that no crime has been committed. Haven't you ever heard of trespassing?

WARD I merely walked into my sister's villa, which incidentally half belongs to me, through those windows, which were open. Since then, nobody has laid a finger on you, nor harmed a hair of your pretty little head. So what is there to fear?

OLIVIA It's just not knowing what's going on (*She is on the edge of tears now*)

WARD Perhaps the time has come for us to have our little talk.

OLIVIA Little talk? What about?

WARD About diamonds. The Transvaal Diamond Corporation . . . and the late McKenzie Prescott.

OLIVIA *throws down some flowers in her hand and angrily starts to move towards the french windows.* WARD *stops her, seizing her wrist.*

WARD No, Olivia . . . you're not going out of here until we've talked about the diamonds. You know which ones. Ten million pounds worth stored in the Company's vaults in Johannesburg; stock-piled over many years, almost Father's entire lifetime.

Olivia has paused and turned back, as Ward lets go of her wrist.

OLIVIA All right. What about the diamonds?

A pause.

WARD You know as well as I do about the Company scandal — and the take-over by an American group . . . but that wasn't why Father killed himself, was it, Olivia?

OLIVIA Father? Are you talking about my father or yours? (*Suddenly sharp*) If it's mine, I'd like to know what the hell it has to do with you? It's all over now anyway, a year ago.

WARD It's not quite all over, Olivia. Let's go back to the time the new Company took over, the American consortium that bought up the shares. Try and imagine it. They have taken control — they have the share certificates in their hands. But what they want to see is the Corporation's assets. Diamonds. So they go to the vaults and what do they find? Nothing. The vaults have been cleaned out. Empty. The biggest diamond haul in history. The Corporation's shares have become worthless. Where are those stones now, Olivia? You didn't sell them did you? We'd know if you had. What did you do with them?

A very long pause.

OLIVIA They simply disappeared. Nobody knows where they are. Nobody . . .

WARD . . . except you, Olivia. Shortly after father's suicide, you booked a flight from Johannesburg to New York, didn't you? Your ticket was booked via London but you never arrived in London, did you? Because you cancelled that flight and flew to Lisbon instead. You must remember that, come on?

Olivia says nothing.

WARD Very well; perhaps later, when you've had a little time to reflect. Take your time.

WARD goes out to the terrace and down the steps. OLIVIA sighs with resignation and continues to arrange the flowers in the vase on the piano. Voices can be heard outside. Suddenly MRS WHITMAN hurries in by the front door, alarmed and breathless.

MRS WHITMAN Ward ... oh ...

She sees OLIVIA and stops short. OLIVIA looks alarmed. She backs away from the piano and stares at the door. Now CARLOS appears and remains by the door as VARGAS walks in.

VARGAS (*Coming in*) May I intrude just once more, Señorita. I seem myself to be the intruder now.

OLIVIA (*Drily*) What is it?

VARGAS A visitor for you.

CHARLES BRINTON comes in. OLIVIA sees him, seems for a moment stunned. Then she lets out a shout of excitement and joy.

OLIVIA Uncles Charles! Oh thank God ... at last

She runs to him and throw herself into his arms, half laughing, half sobbing with sheer relief.

OLIVIA (*Hysterical outpourings*) I've been so desperate and scared ... only you could help me ... I tried ... so hard to get you last night but your phone was off the hook ... then these people said I wasn't here when I was and ...

CHARLES I know ... I know ... the Comisario told me ... there, there ... it's all right now ... we'll soon find out what it's all about ...

OLIVIA ... it's been the most horrible nightmare ... I though I was going round the bend ... literally out of my ... mind with this man who ... keeps on and on saying he's ...

WARD has now walked in through the window from the terrace. CHARLES looks up and sees him. WARD looks at CHARLES.

WARD Uncle Charles, there you are at last.

CHARLES *lets go of* OLIVIA *and moves over to look at him, incredulous.*

CHARLES (*Now recognizing him*) WARD, my dear boy.

OLIVIA *is stunned, as the curtain falls.*

ACT TWO

Scene One

Early evening, a few hours later. The sun is going down and the hall of the villa is getting dark. WARD *and Uncle* CHARLES *are sitting together in silence.* WARD, *aware of the failing light, gets up to switch on a lamp. Uncle* CHARLES *looks at his watch, as he glances at a piece of paper in his hand.*

CHARLES She's taking her time.

WARD Elaine gave her a pretty powerful sedative. A cup of black coffee'll soon bring her round.

CHARLES Let's hope she's making sense. Or will.

WARD After a shock like that, it's anybody's guess. In her delicate state of mind . . .

CHARLES We'll need her signature on this document among others. (*He hands it to* WARD).

WARD We'll get it. Ah . . .

OLIVIA*'s bedroom door opens and* MRS WHITMAN *comes out, escorting* OLIVIA, *who looks very pale and shocked and rather tousled, wearing pyjamas.*

MRS WHITMAN (*Like a nurse*) I think we're ready to talk now, aren't we?

The two men get up and OLIVIA *is steered into a chair. She looks hard at* CHARLES.

OLIVIA (*Rather weakly*) I thought you were the only person in the whole world that I could trust.

CHARLES *turns to* WARD.

CHARLES I think it's time you explained things to her, don't you, Ward?

WARD I'll try. (*To* OLIVIA) Let's pick it up where we left off this afternoon, shall we? (OLIVIA *looks bewildered*). We know you flew to Lisbon soon after the funeral in Pretoria. Perhaps you'd like to tell us where you went on to from there?

A pause. OLIVIA *thinks and answers slowly.*

OLIVIA I went on to America; you know that.

CHARLES Yes?

OLIVIA — But I changed my plans slightly when I got to Lisbon. I rested there for a couple of days. Then . . . well, then I caught a plane on to New York.

WARD — Two days later. Are you quite sure?

OLIVIA — Of course I'm sure. I went straight on to New York.

MRS WHITMAN — You didn't. Not until twelve days later. TWA Flight 903.

OLIVIA — What are you talking about?

WARD — We are still talking about diamonds, Olivia. Ten millions worth once locked away in the vaults of The Transvaal Diamond Corporation, Father's Company.

OLIVIA — (*Very calm*) I'm afraid you're wasting your time. Those diamonds are lost. Nobody will ever find them. Nobody.

MRS WHITMAN — What about the Anglo-Hispano Bank in Tangiers?

OLIVIA — (*Suddenly shocked*) The what?

WARD — Tangier. That's where you went, didn't you? From Lisbon.

OLIVIA *seems momentarily thrown. She thinks hard.*

OLIVIA — All right. Yes. I went to Tangier.

CHARLES — Why?

OLIVIA — Because it happens to be one of the few places in the world, where no one can get at a Bank deposit, even through International Law. But just in case you've forgotten, I signed the deposit slip for those stones. And only my signature can get them out.

CHARLES — That's right, my dear. Only your signature can get them out.

WARD — Come on, Olivia. You must have known you couldn't get away with it. What on earth were you thinking of?

OLIVIA What are you thinking of, that's more to the point. You two, whoever you are, and my two-faced greedy, uncle. Do you think you're going to get away with it? What's the idea? To get the diamonds back and hand them over to the Transvaal Corporation with apologies for the inconvenience, so their shares can pick up again on the Stock Exchange? I doubt it. More likely sell them in Tangier, split the proceeds three ways and scatter.

CHARLES This is quite hopeless. Why don't we let the police decide?

WARD You wouldn't want that, would you, Olivia?

OLIVIA *reflects. A long pause. Then* OLIVIA *becomes suddenly resolved.*

OLIVIA All right. If I do what I know you want me to do, will you promise to go away, all of you, and leave me alone? That's all I ask. Just to be left alone.

WARD *motions to* MRS WHITMAN, *who takes from him a document, which she sets before* OLIVIA *with a pen outstretched.*

MRS WHITMAN All you have to do is sign . . . your normal signature, dear, just there, and the date . . .

OLIVIA (*Reads*) . . . to the Manager, Anglo-Hispano Bank Ltd., Place Mediterranee, Tangier . . . this will introduce my brother Mr Ward McKenzie Prescott, who is hereby empowered to act on my behalf as from . . . (*She sighs*) O.K. Anything for a quiet life.

She signs and dates. MRS WHITMAN *takes the document and hands it to* WARD. CHARLES *gets up to go.*

CHARLES That was sensible, Olivia. Thank you, my dear.

CHARLES *goes to the front door and* MRS WHITMAN *goes out with him to see him off.*

MRS WHITMAN Just a word before you go . . .

CHARLES Certainly.

They exit together. It is darker now. OLIVIA *sits in her chair, staring ahead, dazed.*

WARD I'd pop back into bed now if I were you. Try and get some more sleep. You'll feel better in the morning.

OLIVIA Sleep? Yes, I shall sleep all right. But what about you? I'd have thought you'd find it hard to sleep peacefully in your bed; or haven't you got a conscience about all the lies you've been telling. How can you live with yourself?

WARD Easily. I have nothing to hide.

OLIVIA Yes, you have. Your real identity, for one thing.

WARD I know who I am and so does Uncle Charles, so why the hell don't you?

OLIVIA (*Quietly*) Because I saw my brother after he was dead.

WARD And you're absolutely sure it was . . . him

OLIVIA It was Ward.

WARD I see. Very well.

OLIVIA Now that you've forced me to sign that release for the bank, I trust you and your lady friend will be going away from here and leaving me in peace — as I asked.

WARD We'll see.

OLIVIA If you go to Madrid tonight, you can fly over to Tangier tomorrow, can't you, you two and my dear honest Uncle Charles and collect your loot. (WARD *just smiles*) Well, I'm going to take your advice now and go back to my room to lie down . . . I don't feel very well. Excuse me.

OLIVIA *goes back into her bedroom.* WARD *watches her go. Then* MRS WHITMAN *comes in by the front door.*

MRS WHITMAN Did she have anything to say?

WARD Not much.

MRS WHITMAN I'll take care of that agreement. Might be safer with me. (WARD *hands her the signed document*). Well, what did you talk about?

WARD Conscience, mostly. And sleeping easily with a guilty secret . . She doesn't think I have much of a conscience . . .

MRS WHITMAN In what way?

WARD . . . 'all the lies I tell' . . . she blushed quite prettily, when she said that.

MRS WHITMAN She's a pretty girl. With a lot of charm, when it suits her to use it.

WARD Oh, yes.

MRS WHITMAN Just don't drop your guard, that's all.

WARD Oh, I shan't. Not until we've finished with her.

MRS WHITMAN goes off through the pass door. WARD turns down all the lights and exits by the front door. After a moment OLIVIA's bedroom door-handle turns carefully and she emerges cautiously into the hall. She calls out a bit tentatively:

OLIVIA Carlos! Mrs Whitman!

She goes to the glass windows, which are still open, peers out and calls out across the terrace. We hear a car drive away

OLIVIA Uncle Charles? Mrs Whitman . . .

Now she goes to the front door, opens it and calls down to the drive below. The slight sound of a breeze blowing up . . . might be the mistral. Otherwise, not a sound. OLIVIA closes the front door, laughing quietly to herself, as she comes downstage centre.

OLIVIA All gone now, haven't you? (*Suddenly shouting out loud to nobody in particular*) I knew it. Couldn't wait to get your dirty hands on Father's diamonds, could you? Are you there? Any of you?

Laughing almost hysterically OLIVIA runs over to the pass door and flings it open. She gasps with shock. MRS WHITMAN stands there holding a tray on which is a glass of hot milk and a document.

MRS WHITMAN I heard you calling, Miss Prescott. Would a glass of warm milk help you to sleep perhaps?

OLIVIA (*Recovering and deciding to play it cool*) Oh yes. How kind of you. Thanks.

She takes the milk and puts it down on the piano. Then grabs the document and reads it

OLIVIA Another document to sign? What is it this time (*Reading it aloud*) 'the last will and testament of Olivia Susan Prescott'. I must say, you two do have a macabre sense of humour.

MRS WHITMAN Your brother feels it's time for you to tidy up your affairs, before it's too late.

OLIVIA I see. And where is he, my 'bogus brother'?

MRS WHITMAN Mr Prescott went out in his car for a while. He'll be back later.

OLIVIA I suppose you're his wife, are you? Or do you just occupy the same bed?

MRS WHITMAN *makes no reply but lights a cigarette and calmly walks out through the glass windows on to the terrace and away out of sight.*

OLIVIA (*Calling after her*) You're all plotting to kill me, aren't you? Because I've found out the truth and you've got to make sure I don't . . .

As she goes on talking out loud OLIVIA *first locks the pass door putting the key in her pyjama pocket. Then she crosses to bolt and chain the front door and finally to slide shut and catch the glass windows.*

OLIVIA . . call the police . . . all right go on and do your worst. Kill me, cut my throat or . . . throw me into the sea if you can get in here . . . but I warn you . . . I can look after myself all right . . .

Suddenly a large distorted shadow of a man is thrown against the wall. A man moving slowly towards the villa growing larger each step on the wall. OLIVIA *sees it.*

OLIVIA (*Terrified*) O, my God, no . . .

She backs over to the desk, opens the drawer and gets out the automatic with silencer. She looks wildly round, not sure from which direction the attack will come. Then a sound by the glass windows makes her back away to cover and crouching down by a chair she fires. The dull muffled shot is followed by a crash of broken plate glass. OLIVIA *remains frozen to the spot as a gloved hand reaches in through a hole in the glass panel, uncatches it and slides one side open. With one hand raised* VARGAS *comes into the villa.*

VARGAS (*Angry*) You will hand over that gun at once, Señorita.

OLIVIA *does so.*

VARGAS Thank you. You are a most frightened young lady. Perhaps you will tell my why. I do not believe that shot was intended for me.

OLIVIA (*Very shakey*) No . . . I didn't think . . . it was . . . you . . .

VARGAS It is unwise to shoot at people you cannot see. Who did you imagine I could be?

OLIVIA I don't know. I only know I'm all alone here and terrified . . . thank God you've come.

VARGAS Your Uncle has returned to his villa at San Pedro. The other gentleman has driven into Marbella . . . for some reason.

OLIVIA I've no idea where Carlos is, but the woman is in the garden.

VARGAS *switches on a lamp.*

VARGAS Carlos is in his room and Mrs Whitman is down by the boat-house enjoying a cigarette, so we have a little time but not much.

OLIVIA (*Very tense*) How do you know where everybody is?

VARGAS My dear lady, I am a police inspector. I would be failing in my duty not to have this villa under close observation. Now perhaps you will be good enough to inform me who you imagined you were shooting at and why you are wishing to commit murder.

OLIVIA I was defending myself from . . . the man who calls himself Ward . . . you see he plans to kill me, they all do . . . if you want proof, look at this (OLIVIA *picks up the will from the desk and hands it to* VARGAS) Mrs Whitman brought it to me with a tray of hot milk. They'll force me to sign it . . . and make over everything I possess . . . all that my Father left me in his will . . . to my brother, or rather the man pretending to be . . . my brother. Do you wonder I'm scared out of my wits?

VARGAS (*Glancing at the will*) If you sign this, you will bequeath everything to him. Does that include the diamonds?

OLIVIA What diamonds?

VARGAS . . . belonging to the Transvaal Diamond Corporation.

OLIVIA How did you know about them?

VARGAS My dear lady, every policeman in the world knows about them. How the precious stones disappeared mysteriously, or maybe not so mysteriously . . . in Johannesburg. It was in the newspapers all over the world. (OLIVIA *looks nervously at* VARGAS *but says nothing*) Did you take those diamonds, Señorita Prescott?

OLIVIA (*Shakes her head and moves away from him*) No. Ward stole them from the Corporation vaults. Ward Prescott, my brother.

VARGAS For what reason?

A pause.

OLIVIA As he's dead now, I suppose it doesn't matter very much.

VARGAS So you can tell me.

OLIVIA He was greedy, only interested in having a good time, spending Father's money on girls, gambling and racing cars.

VARGAS Did he owe money?

OLIVIA God, yes. All over the place.

VARGAS How do you know he took the diamonds?

OLIVIA He told me: he boasted how he'd forged my Father's signature on a note to the bank, giving him access to the strong-room.

VARGAS Why did you not go to your father or to the police, when you knew what he was planning?

OLIVIA My Father was in hospital after a mild stroke. If he'd found out that Ward had forged his signature to rob the company of it's main assets, I knew the shock would kill him. The shares bought by the American group would be worthless and my father would be charged with fraud . . .

VARGAS And so . . .

OLIVIA So I tried to persuade Ward to put the diamonds back. But he laughed at me. He was all packed with the stones in a bag in his luggage, ready to drive to the airport and catch a flight to Brazil. He told me he was going to lie low until the heat was off; then start a new life in South America. I begged him not to go . . . pleaded with him. I screamed at him, how could he do this, knowing it might kill his own father but he wouldn't listen. He pushed me out of the way and drove off into the night. I was totally shattered. Then a few hours later the 'phone rang. It was the Pretoria police to say my brother had skidded off the road on his way to the airport: his car had turned over three times and he'd been killed.

VARGAS I see (*Quietly*) And what happened to the stolen diamonds?

OLIVIA I had to go immediately that night to the hospital mortuary in Pretoria . . . and . . . see him . . . identify him . . . they made me sign papers and things and the next morning they gave me his personal belongings taken from the car by the police. I knew the diamonds were in the false bottom of his briefcase, I'd seen him put them there. So . . . I took them out and drove back to Johannesburg, straight to my Father's office.

VARGAS To replace them before their loss was discovered?

OLIVIA (*Nods*) Yes but it was too late . . . (*Becoming upset*) There were already police in the Corporation building when I got there and my father's secretary was in tears. The vault had been found empty and the Fraud Squad were starting an investigation. You see Father's secretary had already been out to the hospital earlier to tell him Ward had been killed and to show him the forged note.

VARGAS And did your father know who forged his signature?

OLIVIA He must have guessed because they found him an hour later lying on the pavement below his private room on the sixth floor. His neck was broken.

VARGAS *nods sympathetically.*

VARGAS And you . . .

OLIVIA I hardly remember anything after I heard the news . . . I think I must have fainted from shock. It's all a kind of blur. When I came to, I realized I still had the diamonds in my possession.

VARGAS And you did not inform the police?

OLIVIA *looks square at* VARGAS.

OLIVIA I couldn't face it . . . I know it was wrong of me not to, but I wanted people to forget the whole thing . . . after all the damage was done, my father was dead and my brother too. Our family name was all over the headlines . . . there was enough scandal . . . so I . . .

VARGAS You ran away, did you not? Where to?

OLIVIA To Tangier. I wanted to deposit the diamonds somewhere absolutely safe . . . then I went on to New York.

VARGAS Was that not rather unwise? To make off with the Corporation assets to which you had no entitlement?

OLIVIA Yes, I know it was wrong. But I was sick and confused and after the awful shock of Ward . . . and my father . . . I didn't know what I was doing . . . so, you do see, don't you, that this man isn't my brother . . . he can't be, can he?

VARGAS I believe you but . . .

OLIVIA (*Tense*) Yes?

VARGAS I would like you to make me a promise. A little bargain between us.

OLIVIA What do you want me to do?

VARGAS I shall do all I can to help you, if you will undertake to return those stones to the Transvaal Diamond Corporation, as soon as it can be arranged.

OLIVIA Yes, of course I will. I promise I will. But how can you help me? Arrest these people? Stop them going off to Tangier for the diamonds?

VARGAS It will be necessary first to prove that this man travels under a forged passport with false credentials.

OLIVIA He does. I've told you he does.

VARGAS If that is true, he has evidently been most clever. But I have up my sleeve one final test which will be quite conclusive.

OLIVIA Oh? What is that?

VARGAS My dear young lady, I have not been idle. My chief in Madrid has today made some enquiries in Pretoria and Johannesburg about your brother. It seems he was in some trouble with the police there four years ago. There was a wild party after the Grand Prix at Kyalami and premises were broken into. A number of young men and women were suspected and finger-prints were taken. Your brother's among them. Madrid received this afternoon copies of those finger-prints . . .

OLIVIA So . . . if this man's prints don't match the ones from South Africa . . .

A long pause.

VARGAS Exactly. Now I shall slip away into the shadows, Señorita Prescott; but do not fear, I shall be watching over you from the darkness outside. When your intruder returns, offer him a drink; then find some way to place his glass outside on the terrace, where I will find it.

VARGAS Naturally, he must not suspect what you do so . . . be very careful. (VARGAS *is about to go. He hesitates and turns, shows her the gun*) One more thing. I am not happy to leave you without any means of self-defence: but it will be wiser if I keep this . . . just for the moment.

VARGAS *slips out through the glass windows and vanishes.* OLIVIA *looks thoughtful and just a bit puzzled. She goes to the drinks trolley and picks up two brandy glasses and a fairly empty bottle of cognac. She pours one for herself and addresses an unseen imaginary companion.*

OLIVIA Would you care to join me in a glass of brandy, Ward dear, before you go up to bed? Oh, come on, let's . . .

She breaks off looking at the cognac bottle which is all but finished. With a wry face she puts down the bottle, goes over the unlock the pass door, finding the key in her pyjama pocket. Then she goes to a wall bell and rings. Next she glances at herself in a mirror and decides to put on some seductive music on the music centre. She restarts the tape of Ravel's Violincello Concerto. Next she mimes disapproval of the way she is dressed in her pyjamas. So she puts down her glass of brandy and goes off into her bedroom, switching on the light. After a moment CARLOS *comes in through the pass door in answer to the bell and looks about him. No sign of* OLIVIA *so he is about to go out when* OLIVIA*'s head and shoulders are seen round the bedroom door.* OLIVIA *is changing her dress.*

OLIVIA Is that you, Carlos?

CARLOS (*Seeing her*) Señorita . . .

OLIVIA Fetch another bottle of Cognac from the cellar, please, and something to clean up that broken glass.

CARLOS Si, Señorita.

CARLOS goes out. OLIVIA comes out of her bedroom, finally zipping herself up into a pretty sexy, sleeveless dress, and wearing her emerald necklace. She quickly fixes her hair and puts on a bit of lipstick, then goes to the drinks trolley again and picking up the empty bottle starts her mime again.

OLIVIA . . . 'would you care to join me in a glass of brandy.' (*To herself*) No, that's too formal . . . 'I say, do have a glass of brandy with me.'

CARLOS has entered unseen by OLIVIA with a bottle and a dustpan and brush.

CARLOS (*Politely*) The Señorita is very kind but I do not drink Cognac . . .

OLIVIA (*Turning and seeing him*) Oh, don't you? Never mind. Just leave the bottle there and sweep up.

CARLOS (*Bowing*) Señorita . . .

He sweeps up the broken glass and watches OLIVIA fingering her necklace, as she completes her toilette, listening to the music. Finally CARLOS goes. Suddenly someone starts banging on the front door and rattling the handle. OLIVIA at first alarmed, realizes it must be WARD, so goes over to unbolt and unchain it. WARD comes in.

WARD What are you doing up?

OLIVIA I couldn't sleep after all. Felt like something to drink. Brandy, I thought.

WARD Brandy will keep you awake.

OLIVIA I feel like something to . . . buck me up a bit. I'm quite wide awake now anyway. How about you?

WARD — No, thanks.

OLIVIA — Oh, please join me. Why not? Celebrate the drafting of my last Will and Testament.

WARD — I'd rather drink to your future.

OLIVIA — Would you really? (OLIVIA *pours two glasses from the new bottle and picks up her own, leaving* WARD*'s on the trolley*) Yours is there. (OLIVIA *sips her brandy*) Phew! It's hot and stuffy tonight. Would you mind opening those windows? Let in a bit of air.

WARD *puts down his glass on the trolley and goes to open the windows. While he has his back turned,* OLIVIA *switches the glasses.* WARD *comes back and takes up the wrong glass, sips it. A silence.*

OLIVIA — You're very quiet tonight.

WARD — Am I?

OLIVIA — Then you don't talk much, do you? Except about unpleasant things.

WARD — Is there anything else for me to talk about?

OLIVIA — There could be . . . no . . . silly of me.

WARD — Under the circumstances . . .

OLIVIA — (*Now holding* WARD*'s glass carefully by the stem*). What if the circumstances were different? If you weren't who you are, what would you think of me, then, I wonder (WARD *remains silent*) It's rather fascinating, isn't it? No, you're not fascinated. Not in the least.

WARD — It's late. Time we locked up.

OLIVIA — I'm going to finish my brandy outside where it's cool. No need for you to come. I'm not going to run away. Just . . . have a bit of fresh air.

OLIVIA *begins to back away upstage to the windows, still holding* WARD*'s brandy glass carefully. Moving with her back to the terrace in order to ensure that* WARD *is not going to follow her from the bar, where he has picked up his [her] glass she finally steps out but, as she turns to face out to the verandah,* MRS WHITMAN *suddenly appears from the steps almost* *running into* OLIVIA, *who lets out a startled, stifled gasp and drops the brandy glass, which shatters on the steps.*

OLIVIA Oh, God. (*To* MRS WHITMAN) I wish you's stop sneaking around like that. You scared me to death.

MRS WHITMAN (*Drily*) I'm so sorry. I've been down by the boathouse. It's cool down there and rather pleasant.

OLIVIA (*Looking down at shattered glass*) What a waste of good brandy.

WARD Get yourself another. You can afford it.

OLIVIA If you say so.

MRS WHITMAN *now moves to the stairs.*

MRS WHITMAN I shall go to bed now, if you'll excuse me, both of you.

OLIVIA Please do.

WARD Goodnight Elaine. Sleep well.

MRS WHITMAN Goodnight, Ward.

MRS WHITMAN *gives* OLIVIA *a look and goes upstairs.*

WARD Well. Aren't you going to give yourself another brandy? I'll bet Uncle Charles stocked the cellar here pretty well. As Father would have. For you.

OLIVIA Would he? (OLIVIA *pours herself another brandy at the drinks trolley*)

WARD Of course he would. You've always had everything you've wanted, haven't you? Being an only daughter; a favourite child with a rich father, who thought the sun shone out of her eyes . . . just as well he didn't live to find out the truth about you.

OLIVIA *puts down her glass on the piano and in a blaze of fury lunges at him with her arm raised. He grabs her arm.*

OLIVIA I ought to hate you more than anyone in the world.

WARD Not half as much as I should hate you. Unfortunately, I rather like you.

OLIVIA *looks hard at* WARD *an enigmatic look. Then, quite quietly she picks up here newly poured glass from the piano and sips it watching him.*

OLIVIA Do you? Well, I'll tell you what I'd rather like.

WARD What?

OLIVIA That tune you played last night, when you first came. Play it for me again, will you? The one you say the pianist used to play in a bar up the coast from Durban.

WARD Oh, that.

OLIVIA Yes. That. Play it for me. Go on.

After a slight hesitation WARD *gets up and goes over to the piano taking his brandy and putting it on the piano. He starts to play.* OLIVIA *stands beside him quite close attempting a little mild seduction. She hums the melody.*

OLIVIA You play it just a fraction faster than Ward used to, more the speed of the pianist in the bar. But that doesn't prove anything, does it?

WARD I don't quite know what you're talking about.

OLIVIA *sips her brandy and puts her glass down very close to* WARD*'s on the piano. He doesn't seem to notice.*

OLIVIA Oh, well, never mind. See if I can pick out the tune. (OLIVIA *leans over the keyboard and with one finger tries to pick out the melody in the treble as* WARD *plays. She gives up with a slight laugh*) Hopeless. I never could play the piano.

She picks up WARD*'s glass leaving her own on the piano and moves away across the room.* WARD *stops playing and gets up.*

WARD Where are you off to?

OLIVIA I don't feel like bed. Not just yet. I may wander down to the pool.

WARD Midnight swim?

OLIVIA I might. (*Pause*) Naked. Like we used to, Ward and I, when we were kids. There's another good reason why you're not my brother. Shall I tell you?

WARD If you want to.

OLIVIA Although we grew up together very close as children. Ward and I, I never felt anything for him, do you know what I mean? Like some sisters do for their brothers. I mean I never found him physically attractive; you know, wanting him to touch me . . .

WARD In other words, you have no incestuous feelings towards me.

OLIVIA I didn't say that.

WARD Didn't you?

OLIVIA Unlike my brother, you see, I do . . . actually find you quite attractive. Just thought you might like to know that . . . you've made a bit of a hit with your victim. I expect you'd guessed. It wasn't unusual for 18th century ladies to fall in love with the highwaymen who stopped their coaches and stripped them of all their jewels.

WARD If you are seeing me as some sort of romantic thief like Raffles or Macheath I do think it's time you went to bed.

OLIVIA At least admit you are some kind of criminal. Come on, don't deny me that little bit of excitement. Please.

WARD Trespass is not a crime unless physical entry is made by force. I believe similar rules apply to incest.

OLIVIA (*Laughing*) How rude. Really.

WARD The analogy was unintentional. I'm sorry.

OLIVIA I don't shock too easily. Is incest a crime? I didn't know it was.

WARD If sexual relations are proved I believe it is an offence.

OLIVIA (*Laughs again*) Sexual relations. What a marvellous description.

WARD It's not really all that funny. You can still go to gaol for it.

OLIVIA Is it a criminal offence for two consenting adults in private?

WARD It depends on what they do and if they get caught.

OLIVIA So whether you were my brother or not and I fancied you and you fancied me, there'd be nothing to stop us making love on a warm Spanish night in a villa by the sea, would there?

WARD Yes. The Law. Now what time do you wish to be called in the morning? I can leave a message for Carlos.

OLIVIA I'm not going to bed. I couldn't possibly sleep. Not now, Mr Whatever Your Name Is.

WARD You know my name.

OLIVIA I don't. All I know is that your presence here, under my roof, rather disturbs me. I do wish we hadn't had that chat about incest. It's put all sorts of ideas into my head. Rather naughty ones, I'm afraid.

WARD Then perhaps you'd better go and plunge into the swimming pool and cool off a bit, before you go to bed.

OLIVIA Yes, perhaps I will go in. Why not come for a skinny dip with me? Come on. There are towels down there. We can dry each other afterwards . . . and . . .

MRS WHITMAN *now comes down the stairs again.*

MRS WHITMAN I hope I'm not interrupting.

OLIVIA Not at all. We were just having a drink and a little music. Did we disturb you?

MRS WHITMAN *does not answer. Instead she looks steadily at* WARD.

MRS WHITMAN I just wondered if you were coming up to bed, that's all. It is rather late.

WARD Yes, it is, isn't it?

OLIVIA *now sees her chance.*

OLIVIA Well, I shall go out and finish by brandy on the terrace, maybe see how the pool feels on my own . . . excuse me . . . oh . . . (*Pausing*) Don't wait up for me.

OLIVIA *goes out on to the verandah and down the steps with her(his) brandy glass.*

MRS WHITMAN (*Urgently*) That was careless of you.

WARD Was it?

MRS WHITMAN Which brandy glass did she take outside, her own or the one with your fingerprints on it?

WARD *looks at her and the penny drops.*

WARD (*Quickly*) Vargas mustn't have those prints. I didn't spend a year planning this thing to have it fouled up by some Spanish copper.

MRS WHITMAN Then we must stop her . . . come on . . . they'll probably meet up on the beach.

They go out quickly. After a second or two OLIVIA *comes furtively in again. Seeing the coast is clear, she slips into her room, and quickly comes out again with her coat and shoulder bag. She runs to the front door, flings it open and gasps with shock.* CHARLES *is there. She gapes at him and tries to rush out past him but he grabs her roughly by the arm.*

CHARLES (*Fiercely*) No, Olivia. I'm afraid I can't allow you to leave this place. Not now.

The lights fade out.

Scene Two

The next morning, early. OLIVIA, *worn out from an all-night grilling, is sitting in a chair.* WARD, MRS WHITMAN *and* CHARLES *are present and there are cups of coffee and cigarette butts in evidence.*

CHARLES Why not be sensible Olivia? We don't want to go through all that distressing business with doctors again.

MRS WHITMAN I do think you'd be wise to co-operate with us, dear.

OLIVIA *says nothing.*

WARD Very well. Then we shall have to use co-ercion. Your bag please. (*No answer.* WARD *raises his voice*) I said the bag. (OLIVIA *clutches her bag close like a scared child.* WARD *and* MRS WHITMAN *exchange looks. At the top of his voice*) Give me that bag. (WARD *goes quickly over to her and rips the bag from her grasp. He opens it. To the others*) I'll give you three guesses what's in it.

CHARLES I think we all know, don't we?

WARD *extracts the contents of the bag putting the items down.*

WARD One set of house keys, one set of car keys, one passport and a lot of pesetas . . . one diamond and emerald necklace . . . very nice.

CHARLES (*Taking it*) I'll say it's nice, and rare too, this emerald's a double-cut cabochon.

WARD And this.

WARD *holds up a small cloth bag tied up at the neck, undoes the string and pours out the contents on to the desk. A cascade of glittering diamonds of all shapes and sizes.*

WARD The biggest diamond haul in history.

CHARLES *picks up one of the diamonds and examines it. Then he puts it back with the rest.*

CHARLES Ten million pounds' worth. It would seem that a journey to Tangier will not be necessary, after all.

OLIVIA (*In a dead, resigned voice*) What are you going to do to me? Please tell me. I'm not afraid . . . I'd just . . . like to know . . . what you're planning to do . . . to me now.

WARD Do to you? What should we do to you?

MRS WHITMAN We want your signature, that's all. On this document.

WARD You must sign and initial your will, Olivia, Elaine and Carlos can witness it.

MRS WHITMAN It won't take a second. Come along, dear. Over here.

OLIVIA *gets up and slowly goes over to the desk. She sits, as before, to sign the will but hesitates.*

CHARLES Is something the matter with that pen? If so, borrow mine.

OLIVIA *shakes her head and looks dazedly at the document.*

OLIVIA It really does seem a little strange . . . to sign a piece of paper leaving everything I inherited from my father to a dead man . . . and to an uncle I used to love so dearly . . . who seems to have taken to crime in his old age. But, if it's what you want, all of you, to rob me of everything I possess and then destroy me like a sick animal, I don't seem to have much choice. Better sign my own death warrant and be damned . . .

OLIVIA *signs the will,* MRS WHITMAN *witnesses it and takes it.* CHARLES, *a bit distressed, perhaps feeling guilty, moves to the terrace and gazes out to sea.*

MRS WHITMAN I'll go and see if Carlos is back; and get him to witness it.

MRS WHITMAN *goes out by the pass door with the will.*

WARD There. It's always nice to get the main business of the day over before breakfast. Especially on a sunny morning like this.

OLIVIA *just stares ahead of her.* CARLOS *now enters through the pass door, followed by* MRS WHITMAN. *He is just handing her back the will and her pen.* WARD *nods to him. He seems to understand and moves over to stand with his back to the front door, as though to guard it.*

WARD (*To* OLIVIA) Now go and sit over there, please.

OLIVIA Why?

WARD (*Very sharp*) Just do as you're told. (*Shouts at her*) Go on. Away from that desk. Move.

OLIVIA *terrified, goes quickly over to sit again on the sofa.* WARD *proceeds to collect the diamonds off the desk, scooping them up carefully and replacing them in the bag.* MRS WHITMAN *comes to stand by him, while he ties up the neck of the bag tightening the cord. Then* WARD *hands the bag to* MRS WHITMAN.

WARD Put these somewhere safe, will you, until we leave.

MRS WHITMAN Yes, very well. I'll take care of them.

MRS WHITMAN *goes off upstairs with the bag of diamonds.* WARD *moves up to the windows and looks out and down towards the sea.* OLIVIA *sits staring at* WARD *and* CHARLES, *terrified.* WARD *turns from the glass windows.*

WARD The sea looks nice and calm this morning. How about a swim, Uncle Charles?

CHARLES No, no. Bit too early in the day for me.

WARD Really? Pity. I'd like someone to come with me. Might get the boat out. It's nice and calm out there. Perfect day for it. Come on, Charles, keep me company.

CHARLES (*Tense*) I'd rather not thank you, Ward. Not today.

WARD *turns to* OLIVIA.

WARD Well, Olivia. I guess you're my only hope. What do you say?

WARD Come on, Olivia, don't let me down. You always used to enjoy swimming out of the boat.

MRS WHITMAN *appears coming down the stairs.*

MRS WHITMAN You'll have to be careful out there. The currents off that point can be quite treacherous.

WARD That's all right. I shall be wearing my Aqualung. Personally. And Olivia is quite a strong swimmer. Aren't you?

CHARLES *seems upset by the conversation and turns his head away, not wanting any part of it. He moves towards the front door.*

CHARLES If you'll excuse me, I'll go down and wait in my car. I'll be out there in case I'm wanted.

CHARLES *goes out of the front door.* WARD *tries again. This time he is sharp and angry.*

WARD Come along, Olivia. I want you to come swimming with me. Pull yourself together.

OLIVIA You're going to drown me, aren't you, in the sea . . . now that I've signed that Will, you all want me dead . . .

WARD Don't talk such utter nonsense. Come on.

OLIVIA No. No! Please not. I don't want a swim . . . not today . . .

WARD *nods quickly to* CARLOS, *who comes over and grabs* OLIVIA *from behind, pinioning her arms and lifting her bodily out of the sofa, heaving her towards the terrace.* OLIVIA *lets out a stifled scream.*

OLIVIA No!

MRS WHITMAN Really, Miss Prescott, it's not as though the water's even cold . . . it'll be lovely this morning, warm as toast.

OLIVIA Let me go . . . I don't want to die . . . no . . .

Suddenly CHARLES *appears again at the front door, looking a bit grave*

CHARLES (*Sharply*) Wait. (*Quieter*) I think you'd better postpone your swim, Ward. Vargas is here.

WARD *motions* CARLOS *to let go of* OLIVIA, *who now runs to the front door, as* VARGAS *comes in with a* GUARDIA *again.* OLIVIA *is crying with fear.*

OLIVIA Help me . . . please . . . save me . . . they're trying to drown me in the sea . . . you must . . . help me . . .

She clutches at VARGAS *but he, gently, repels her.*

WARD (*Cheerfully*) Good-morning, Señor Comisario. We were just having a little argument about going down for a swim. Certain persons regard the water as a wee bit too cold, so a little persuasion seemed in order . . . didn't it, Olivia? Come on, be a brave girl. Or do you want me to chuck you in bodily, like I used to when we were kids, do you remember the times I used to have to chuck you in . . . bodily.

A long silence. WARD *is a bit uneasy.* MRS WHITMAN *turns to look out to the terrace.* OLIVIA *looks at* VARGAS *then makes a move towards* WARD.

OLIVIA (*Suddenly very controlled*) Now then Ward, my dear bogus, fake brother, with your forged passport and your false papers and your painted tattoo mark on your arm, I have news for you. I'm afraid you forgot one important detail. Didn't he Señor Vargas? You forgot to do something about your fingerprints. Tell him Señor Comisario. Go on, tell him . . . and then we'll see who's been lying (VARGAS *is silent*) You must tell him what you've discovered,Señor Comisario. Go on.

A silence, as OLIVIA, *slightly triumphant, waits for* VARGAS *to speak. When he does, his voice is very quiet and matter-of-fact.*

VARGAS I have checked the fingerprints, Señorita; those on the record, sent from Pretoria to Madrid . . .

OLIVIA There you are. You see.

VARGAS . . . with those on the brandy glass, which you kindly placed on the terrace last night.

OLIVIA And . . .

VARGAS They match. They belong to one and the same person. The two sets of fingerprints are identical.

A stunned silence. OLIVIA *stares in disbelief.*

OLIVIA That's impossible . . . that . . . that just can't be . . . they . . . they . . . someone's made a mistake.

VARGAS I have been assured that a double-check was made in Madrid and Pretoria. There can be no mistake. (VARGAS *moves over to* WARD) I trust you will accept my apologies, Señor Prescott. Your sister asked for my help. You will appreciate it was my duty to listen carefully to her story and to carry out certain investigations.

WARD Of course. Understood. Trouble is I was unaware of her state of mind; we had no idea how severe her nervous breakdown had been, how sick she really was. And to what extent she was suffering from delusions.

OLIVIA He's lying. Don't listen to him . . . that's all lies . . .

MRS WHITMAN *goes, nurse-like, to soothe* OLIVIA, *putting an arm around her.*

MRS WHITMAN Now, we mustn't get too excited must we? Please try to keep calm, Miss Prescott.

OLIVIA Let go of me. You know bloody well I'm not ill or mad; you're all trying to kill me . . . for what I possess . . . what you want from me . . . all of you . . . do you think I don't know that?

VARGAS These people are not wishing to kill you, Miss Prescott. I believe they are trying very hard to help you to get well. To restore your state of mind.

WARD (*To* VARGAS) I believe you mentioned a clinic outside Malaga.

VARGAS Yes. Santa Maria del Santos. One of the consultants there is a good friend of mine. Dr Pedro Alvarez: I shall ask him to contact you, if you so wish.

VARGAS *turns as if to go.* OLIVIA *becomes even more distressed.*

OLIVIA Not you too. Oh, God, you can't leave me alone with these people . . . you know they'll kill me . . . can't you see what they're doing . . .

VARGAS I shall telephone Dr Alvarez this morning.

OLIVIA (*To* VARGAS) All right . . . the diamonds. The Trans . . . the Transvaal . . . diamonds . . . I admit it . . . I took them . . . I stole them . . . it was me . . . you can arrest me for that . . . you must . . . and send me to jail . . . I'll be safe there . . . from them.

MRS WHITMAN (*Again consoling her*) Of course . . . we know the diamonds are safe now . . . sh . . . sh . . . calm yourself, Miss Prescott. I'll give her a sedative.

OLIVIA Wait! (*She breaks away from* MRS WHITMAN *and stands facing them all defiantly. Pointing to* WARD) That man . . . can . . . not be my brother. Not possibly. Don't you understand? Because . . . my brother is dead . . . I know he's dead . . . I must know . . . for sure, because . . . I killed him.

A silence. Nobody moves. OLIVIA*'s voice drops down to a flat level tone. She speaks mechanically, as if in a subsconscious state.*

OLIVIA We were having a terrible row, just before he left for the airport. He was drinking heavily and I managed to slip two very strong sleeping pills into his glass; thinking he'd get drowsy at the wheel and pull up. When he drove off I followed him at a distance hoping I could get the diamonds back, while he was drugged in his car. But he didn't stop . . . (OLIVIA *breaks down and sobs hysterically in the ensuing silence*) . . . he drove along at a terrific speed and then I saw his car skid right across the road and somersault down an embankment. I stopped on the hard shoulder and ran down to Ward's car. It was on its side half way across a shallow stream. Ward was hanging out through a smashed window by his safety belt, upside down and pouring with blood from the broken glass but still alive, and trying to say something. I released his belt and he dropped down into the stream with his head under the water . . . I pressed hard on his neck with my foot, until I knew he must have died.

When the Police arrived I told them I'd been following him to say goodbye at the airport, as he was leaving his car there. I killed Ward, you see, because of what he'd done to my father.

Then WARD *nods to* MRS WHITMAN, *who picks up the telephone on the desk.*

MRS WHITMAN (*Cool into phone*) Madrid . . . ocho . . . tres . . . seisenta . . . si . . . gracias. (*Someone answers and* MRS WHITMAN *hands the receiver to* WARD) Your number.

WARD *takes the phone.*

WARD (*Into phone*) Hullo . . . Madrid, Police Headquarters . . . Comisario Rojas, please. (*Pause*) Detective Inspector Williams here, South African Police. Yes. That's right. (*While he waits on the line* WARD *turns to* VARGAS) Sorry we couldn't let you in on this before. We had very strict orders from Pretoria. Too many of us knowing might have blown it.

VARGAS You were only just in time, sir. Last night, I believed her story.

WARD I know you did. (*Into phone*) Comisario Rojas? Williams here. Yes we're out at the villa now. We've got a confession out of her in front of witnesses. Would you telex at once to Pretoria for an extradition order. Sorry it took so long. Had to resort to somewhat irregular methods, but she cracked in the end . . . yes . . . Thank you.

WARD *hangs up and makes a sign to* MRS WHITMAN *who goes quickly upstairs.* VARGAS *moves over to* WARD *and speaks quietly.* CHARLES *goes to* OLIVIA *who looks at him.*

OLIVIA Why you?

CHARLES I happened to be very fond of your brother. (*Pause*) I'll see that they get a good lawyer for you. The best that money can buy . . . you must be very brave and sensible. Come along now and let's get you properly dressed. You'll have to go with them.

CHARLES *helps* OLIVIA *to her feet and supports her as she limps painfully towards her bedroom.* MRS WHITMAN *comes back down the stairs with the bag of diamonds.*

OLIVIA (*Brokenly*) It was too late but I did it . . . for my father . . . only for him . . . because I loved him . . . it was only for him.

MRS WHITMAN *hands the bag of diamonds to* WARD.

MRS WHITMAN Do you believe that?

WARD *looks at the bag of diamonds in his hand, then at* CHARLES *and* OLIVIA *who are moving towards the bedroom.*

WARD Do you?

CURTAIN

PROPERTY LIST PLOT

DESK SET WITH	Box of matches. Lamp. Brass Tub full of cigarettes. Table lighter. Brass Box. Magic Pen. *Olé* Magazine (with Olivia's Picture). Phone. Photo of Ward. White Onyx Ashtray.
SET IN D.S. DRAWER	Gun set d.s. end. Torch.
COFFEE TABLE	Oblong tray set with 2 dirty glasses & white cloth. Avante Garde Magazine. 1 Dirty Glass. Glass Astray. Brass Dish & *Olé* Magazine.
PIANO	3 Dirty Glasses. White Onyx Ashtray. Vase set with Roses and Filler. Piano lid open.
DRINKS CABINET	4 Tumblers. 3 Whiskey Glasses. 1 Whiskey Glass. 1 Brandy Glass. Jug of Sangria - $\frac{3}{4}$ full. Cocktail Shaker with lid set behind. Brandy Bottle - Almost empy. Whisky Bottle - Half Full. Noilly Pratt. Gin. Cassis. Glass & Bottle dressing underneath. Lamp. White pottery ashtray. Soda Siphon. Ice Bucket & Lid. Ice Tongs.

	Cocktail Spoon. Black Dish set with slices of orange & lemon. Cloth set by ashtray. J Cloth set hidden on shelf. 1 Cassette in deck. 1 Cassette loose on shelf. Book & Record Dressing.
PATIO	TABLE set with 3 dirty glasses. CHAIR 2 Dirty Glasses set in recess. 1 Dirty Glass set U.S.C.
D.S.L. PROPS TABLE	Handbag set with - House Keys. Pesetas. Bag Of Diamonds. N.B. Car Keys & Necklace to be set in Interval. Tissues. Water & Beakers. CHECK Wood Splint Effect. Coffee Cup & Saucer.
U.S.L. QUICK CHANGE AREA	Ward's Glasses set in cream jacket pocket. Clothes preset for Quick Change - Trousers. Shirt. Shoes. Jacket. Ashtray + water. Water & Beakers & Tissues. Goggles, Gloves & hammer.
U.S.L. PROPS TABLE	Thermos of Coffee. Round Tray set with Coffee Pot & Milk Jug. 1 Coffee Cup & Saucers. Broom.
U.S.R. PROPS TABLE	Bunch of Flowers. Brandy Glass wrapped in hankey. Water Spray. CHECK GRAVEL BOX. + 2 Keys set off-stage by Front Door.
D.S.R. PROPS TABLE	Full Brandy Bottle. Dustpan & Brush.

Metal Bowl.
First Aid Box set with TCP Bottle, Swabs & plasters.
Magic Pen.
A few pesetas.
Last Will & Testament.
Glass of Milk.
Large Screwdriver.
Matches and cigarette.
Letter of Introduction.
Postcard.
Set of Keys (& Jacket).
Tray set under table for prop glasses.

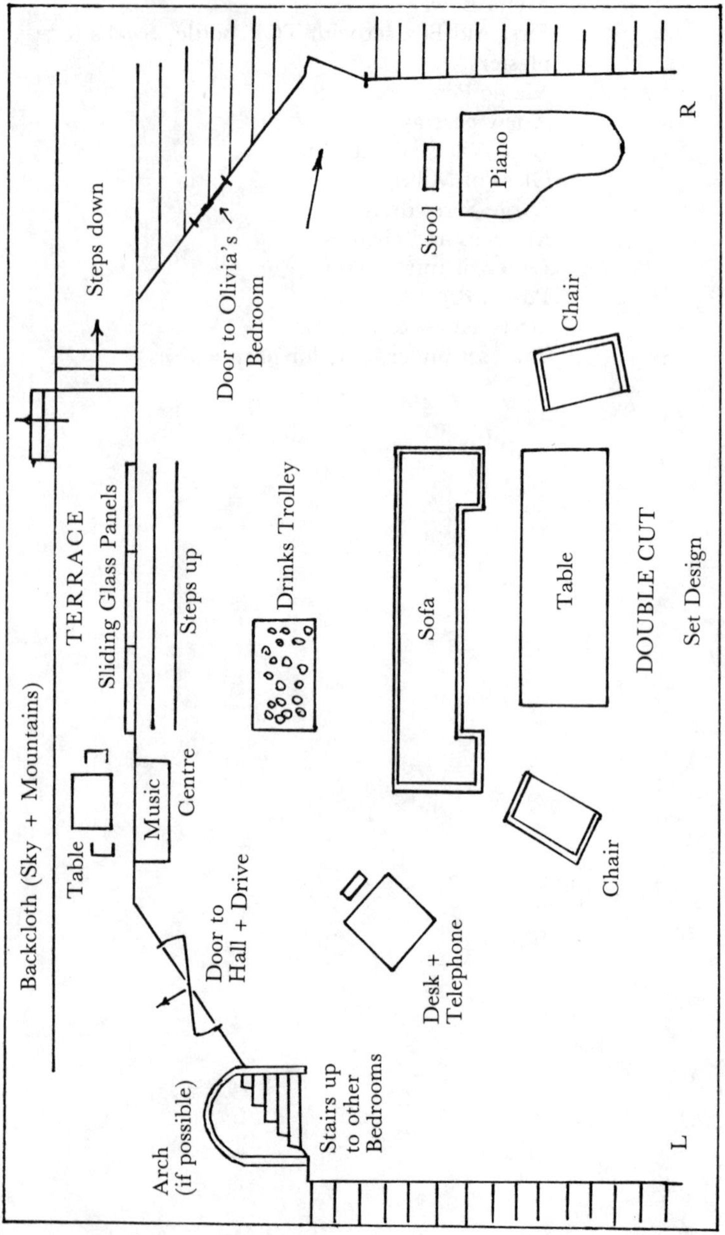

Backcloth (Sky + Mountains)
TERRACE
Table
Sliding Glass Panels
Steps down
Music
Centre
Steps up
Drinks Trolley
Door to Olivia's
Bedroom
Door to
Hall + Drive
Arch
(if possible)
Stairs up
to other
Bedrooms
Desk +
Telephone
Sofa
Table
Chair
Chair
Stool
Piano
DOUBLE CUT
Set Design
L
R

Monde